FRANK MEADOW SUTCLIFFE

Hon F.R.P.S

Whitby and its people as seen by one of the founders of the naturalistic movement in photography.

A second selection of his work compiled by Bill Eglon Shaw.

The Sutcliffe Gallery,
Whitby, North Yorkshire,
England.

First Published 1978

The Lithoprinter Magazine Award for Overall Excellence
and The Crabtree Trophy for Presswork — 1979

First re-printed 1982 with some improvements
Second re-print 1985
Published and © 1985 by:

The Sutcliffe Gallery
1 Flowergate, Whitby, North Yorkshire, YO21 3BA,
England   Tel: (0947) 602239

by agreement with Whitby Literary & Philosophical Society

The book printed by
Jayscale Duotone Offset at
the printing house of
Hawthornes Leeds
formerly John S. Speight Limited
Parkside Works, Guiseley, Leeds LS20 8BH

Limited Edition   0 9503175 5 1   (now fully subscribed)
Hard Cover General Edition   0 9503175 4 3   (out of print)
Soft Cover General Edition   0 9503175 3 5

INTRODUCTION

Since 1974 when we published the first book containing a selection of photographs taken by Frank Meadow Sutcliffe other collections of negatives and prints by early photographers have come to light coincidentally with several books which have been produced on the subject of nineteenth century photography. These have only served to confirm Sutcliffe's stature in this field and to establish him amongst the few true masters of photography.

Although we are daily printing and hand finishing photographs from his original negatives we never lose our sense of respect and admiration for the exquisite artistry and craftsmanship which it is our privilege to re-create on present-day materials using, possibly, more sophisticated methods than were available to Sutcliffe. Whether, having access to such methods, prints of superior quality are produced by us than were made in Sutcliffe's own time is open to question.

There are times when we feel that a negative has been interpreted in such a way that it would be difficult to imagine anything superior, but also occasions when we have a suspicion that we may not have done full justice to the subtlety of the image — such is the sensitivity required when printing these negatives.

Just as a contemporary orchestral conductor has had no first hand experience of how the nuances of Beethoven's works were intended to be interpreted and must therefore use his own experience and creative instincts in performances of his work, so we have to re-create, as near as we are able, the intentions and messages suggested in the photographic negative.

Scarcely any of the prints which we make are 'straight' — but almost always involve holding back a shadow area here or bringing gradation into a near highlight there, together with the variations introduced by the control of image contrast and tonal depth. But in one respect alone we are in a more fortunate position than the orchestral conductor in that (in some instances) we have actual early prints made by Sutcliffe to which to refer.

Although not concerned with the introduction of variables the process of hand finishing is worth describing. It is necessary to bring our prints up to the immaculate standard which Sutcliffe set himself when exhibiting his work.

When a photograph is printed from an early negative the resulting print invariably bears a number of imperfections in the form of white spots or scratches (blemishes which would print as black spots are previously "spotted out" on the negative). We remove these by the painstaking and meticulous process of matching each one to its surrounding image depth by the use of a keen eye and steady hand combined with a fine pointed sable-haired brush and photographic dye. To make them suitable for reproduction many of the prints used when illustrating this book each took several hours of careful work.

As mentioned in our previous book Frank Sutcliffe left us his magnificent photographs but very little in the way of informative facts relating to them — indeed in the main they require no additional commentary. However, as many readers of this book will have had no personal contact with this isolated part of the world we have attempted to add interesting information wherever this has been available and we thank the many people who over the years have given us these details. Particular thanks are given to Miss Kathleen Corner of Whitby, Frank Sutcliffe's niece, for help in identifying Sutcliffe's children and to Mr D. G. Sythes for recognising and describing many of the maritime subjects.

The printing process by which the book has been produced is duotone offset lithography. "Duotone" in this context indicates that the photographs are reproduced from two plates: one to record the mid and high tones and the other to give strength and gradation in the shadow areas. We have been extremely fortunate in finding a printer who understands the objectives and execution of this process when applied to the reproduction of monochrome photography.

Having hopefully, given a greater insight into what our activities involve we now present the latest selection, the majority of the photographs not previously having been published — many of them in fact have not yet been exhibited in our Gallery.

Whitby town and lower harbour from the east cliff. Probably the most dramatic photograph in the collection of work by Frank Meadow Sutcliffe, this is an early copy negative and the impressionistic effect could well be the result of having used a bromoil print as an intermediate from which the copy was made.

It is easy to imagine why Bram Stoker set a substantial part of the 19th century novel ''Dracula'' in the ancient port of Whitby.   E-26B.

Whitehall Ship Yard with the North Eastern Railway Company's goods yard on the left. A ship building yard has existed on this site since the 18th century.   26-21A.

One of the many wrecks which were a common sight on the beaches of the North Sea coast during the sailing era. Taken on Whitby beach near Upgang.   A-45C.

"Winter Sunset". A serene and peaceful view across Whitby upper harbour.   24-35B.

'Cud' Colley — a Whitby fisherman.   16-48B.

Sutcliffe was no great lover of steam tugs — largely because of the filthy smoke emitted from their boilers burning low-grade coal. Taken in Whitby lower harbour, a Lowestoft registered lugger is moored at the left against the harbour wall with the tandem-funnelled paddle tug "Guide" near her. On the right is the "Cleveland", a paddle tug owned by the North Eastern Railway Co. and built at South Shields in 1881.

One of the most blemished negatives in the collection and because it verges on under-exposure, also one of the most difficult from which to make an acceptable print.   11-38G.

This tranquil view of Whitby upper harbour shows Cornish luggers from Penzance in the mid distance at left and herring mules with an assortment of trading ketches in the background. The boats in the foreground are Whitby cobles.   4-23C.

Anna Mary Middlemas of Whitby — a studio portrait.   3-68D.

"Fisher Boy". A studio portrait of James Gray who was killed in the first World War. Born in 1879, this photograph would be taken circa 1890. He married Ada Eglon who bore him eight children.   24-33E.

"The Skipper and the Mate". Two old salts, probably taken aboard a trading vessel. 26-35B.

A group of fisherpeople at Coffee House Corner where fish auctions were held. On the photograph is Hannah Hall and Hannah Gildroy. For this location see also 3-84B (p. 31). 19-39B.

An almost theatrical composition. The eight fishergirls have been carefully arranged on the steps at the foot of Whitby's east pier. E-6C.

Whitby fishermen on Tate Hill pier. 4th and 5th from left are Tom Storr and John 'Batch' Batchelor.   24-5A.

Fish stall on New Quay Road, Whitby, with Tom Gaines, his wife Dolly and Anna Ward.   4-18B.

Pier Road, Whitby before the fish quay was widened in the early part of this century. From a glass half plate copy negative, the original for which was probably exposed on early Kodak rollfilm.   31-8G.

Fishermen on Whitby east pier. Although noise may have increased due to the growth in technology, hob-nail boots on the cobble-stoned streets of Victorian towns must have contributed their own distinctive background to life in those times.   2-52B.

Upper harbour, Whitby with Scottish "Fifies", and in the centre a "Zulu" with her nets drying on a spar rigged between the two masts. A scene redolent of peaceful summer days and smells of the sea.   B-44A.

Low tide, Bog Hall, Whitby upper harbour. Taken in 1891, it shows a brigantine and a partially rigged trading ketch with a three masted barque in the background.   13-45A.

An unidentified barquentine in Whitby upper harbour. She is certainly a very trim vessel with a fine figurehead and was probably used in the timber trade. Note the spike bowsprit. A white painted steam yacht is just visible in the left-hand middle distance. Herring barrels are on the quayside at left.   17-20B.

Fishermen and boys in cobles at the foot of harbourside steps on Marine Parade, Whitby. The man third from left is wearing what was known as a "gaff top'sl hat". The boat on the right is a typical 17 foot sailing coble, probably locally built.   B-31C.

A delightfully lively photograph and a difficult one to attempt with a whole plate stand camera. It shows a Penzance registered lugger in Whitby lower harbour. The use of small wooden casks as net floats is of interest as is the long mizzen outrigger.   17-21D.

Cornish luggers ''Hope'' and ''Glance'' moored against the New Quay, Whitby. The Cornish fishing fleet fished off the west Cornish coast for mackerel and pilchard, and along the Irish sea for herring. After passing through the Caledonian Canal into the North Sea, they followed the herring shoals as they moved south, landing their catches at Whitby and Scarborough in September and October. This practice continued up to the first World War.   17-14C.

Two Whitby fisher lasses. Taken on the Scaur, a rocky beach near Whitby east cliff.   11-39C.

One of the earliest photographs in the collection. From a wet plate negative. Location uncertain.   D-9B.

Fisherwomen against the harbour rails at Whitby.   B-29D.

A vegetable cart at the bottom of Pier Road. The building to the left (since demolished) was at that time the Neptune Inn.   E-8B.

Taken on Tate Hill Pier in Whitby lower harbour. Of interest is the baited fishing line, known as a 'long line', near the fisherman's feet. 13-15C.

One of Sutcliffe's more obviously posed studies but nevertheless possessing its own charm. Brother and sister taken on the beach at Whitby. 20-15D.

Titled "Dolce Far Niente" or literally, "It is good to do nothing". An imaginative and unconventional grouping.   6-88A.

The girl at left is knitting a gansey pattern fisherman's pullover whilst one from a jersey design is being knitted by the right hand side girl. The gansey being knitted would be to an authentic Whitby pattern.   20-45A.

The two women winding wool are wearing the bonnets characteristic of the North Yorkshire coast. Each village had its own slight variation in pattern.   E-5D.

A rather contrived shot at Bog Hall on the lower reaches of the Esk. 'Stumper' Dryden (so called because of his wooden leg) is seated on the anchor.   20-44A.

An unidentified top'sl schooner in Whitby upper harbour, moored to the wooden quay owned by the North Eastern Railway Co. The boats in the background are herring mules and sailing cobles. The coble W.Y. 178 "Toiler of the Sea" can be seen with a sloping mast and built "three planks to the water line". She was probably Northumberland built as is shown by the flattened forepeak. 19-26B.

A thriving period for Whitby! A fish auction being held at Coffee House Corner along Pier Road. A point of interest is the tricycle perambulator next to the horse and cart, the latter being loaded with empty herring barrels.   3-84B.

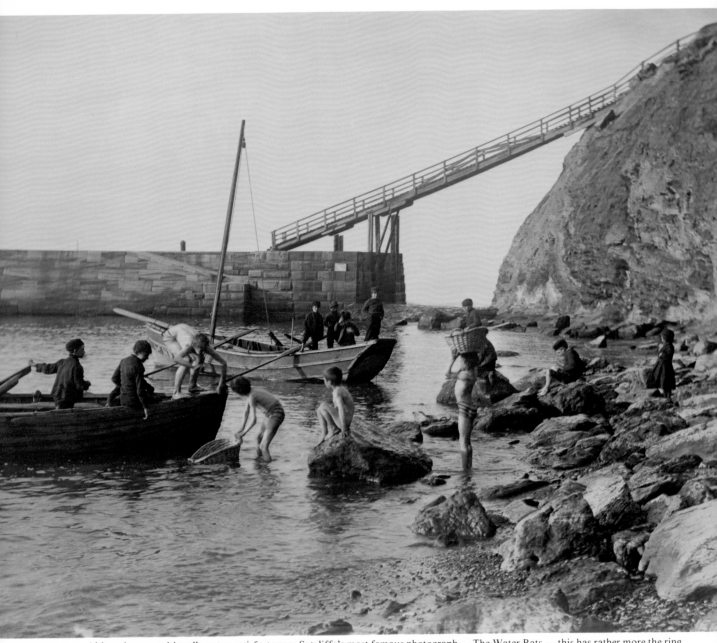

Although compositionally not as satisfactory as Sutcliffe's most famous photograph — The Water Rats — this has rather more the ring of truth about it. The children are arranged more haphazardly and for this reason one has the feeling that (although almost certainly carefully arranged) it is a spontaneous exposure. The original negative is extremely discoloured and blemished and yet curiously yields a surprisingly good print. D-35C.

Whitby Dock End in the upper harbour. One of Sutcliffe's favourite locations. From this photograph it is not difficult to see why. With its wealth of activity, human interest and ever-changing maritime scene, Whitby at that time must surely have been a photographer's paradise.

The main subject is a Berwick registered herring drifter with a high peaked lugsail, mast stepped right forward and outrigger boom aft. On the left is the coal hulk "The George" and in the background a Middlesbrough registered steam trawler and "Dandy", a Whitby yawl. 12-41A.

The pair of Whitby ''yawls'' in the right mid distance were to be ousted by steam trawlers during the early 1900s but these locally built, ketch rigged boats with loose footed mainsails and stump mainmasts were fishing locally between 1870 and 1905. They carried a coble on the maindeck. The practice of hanging washing to dry over the upper harbour was commonplace at that time. 6-55B.

During Sutcliffe's time Whitby's reputation as a holiday resort began to grow and some of the local fishermen saw the possibilities which this new influx of wealth presented.

This is Pier Road, facing onto the harbour and the notice boards on the facia of the house announce that John Douglas (upper board) and Thos. Thompson, both pilots, were offering boats for hire for fishing parties and excursions on both coast and river. 16-14B.

Winter in Whitby, St. Hilda's Terrace under snow. This view has changed little since Sutcliffe's time. The iron railings on the left were taken as scrap metal during World War II and the boundary wall at right has been demolished and re-built to allow some road-widening to take place.   10-10B.

Ruswarp Mill on the River Esk. A flour mill has existed on this site since 1752 when it was built to the order of Nathaniel Cholmley, Lord of the Manor of Whitby. In the 1850s Thos. H. Hay owned and managed the mill and it subsequently passed into the hands of his son and grandson. During severe winters ice skating was possible at this point on the river.   10-46A.

One of Whitby's oldest streets, Sandgate dates back to the early fifteenth century. In the days when smugglers had the support of many local people and smuggling was a lucrative pastime, this was the scene of much violence when contraband goods captured by Revenue Officers were being taken to the Custom House located in Sandgate.   13-41D.

St. Mary's Parish Church as seen through the West Door of Whitby Abbey. This arch was destroyed by German gun-fire in 1914. 16-42A.

Interior of St. Mary's Parish Church. Dating in part from around 1100 AD, the structure has been added to over the centuries. The triple deck pulpit and 'horse-box' pews are of interest.   24-46D.

Building the Whitby to Stockton railway at Sandsend, circa 1874.   27-5C.

Laying the first electricity cable under the River Esk at Bog Hall ford, circa 1910.   25-39A.

The brick built caissons forming the foundations for the Whitby to Scarborough railway viaduct which was built around 1882. Note the steam powered crane and the diver in his — by present standards — primitive suit.   27-4B.

Many of Sutcliffe's photographs were taken at Staithes, about nine miles north west along the coast from Whitby. The cliff in the background is Cowbar Nab with 'ploshers' (the colloquial name for the type of fishing boats more generally known as cobles) in the harbour which at that time was almost unprotected. There are now stone-built jetties to break the full force of the sea.

Some of the boats in the photograph are Northumberland built whilst those with the more up-curved forepeaks would originate in Whitby. 18-8C.

The Openings, one of the narrow "gunnels" in Robin Hood's Bay, a coastal village five miles south east of Whitby. Shirley House, shown here was built in 1651 and is shown on the deeds as costing just over £100 when new. The old man is Stephen Cooper.   20-12A.

Staithes at the foot of Cowbar Bank. One wonders whether Sutcliffe's subjects, who to us now appear such individualistic characters, were so viewed in their own day.   19-45B.

Mrs Longster of Staithes. From an early copy negative. Note the beautifully crocheted shawl. This photograph was taken on the Staith (the elevated flat area separating houses and sea). The low construction on which Mrs Longster is leaning was built in an attempt to deflect the full force of the sea away from the houses during exceptionally high tides.   19-46F.

Titled "Retired from the Sea". Isaac Verrill of Staithes.   3-78D.

Characters such as Isaac Verrill, who appears in this photograph, together with the picturesque houses and alleyways of Staithes, made the place a Mecca for artists. At one time the village attracted a group of painters which included Laura Knight (later to become Dame Laura). The group derived much of its inspiration from the North Yorkshire coastline and its fishing communities. 3-82A.

"November". From an early half plate copy negative which is most likely to have been made from a Kodak rollfilm negative taken around 1900. Thought to have been taken along Eskdaleside, a country lane about four miles from Whitby. 31-1D.

"Last Load of the Day". Probably taken somewhere in the Esk Valley.   10-14E.

"Hurricane Corner, Lealholm". The original exposure was probably on early Kodak rollfilm which was copied by Sutcliffe onto the half plate glass negative from which this was reproduced.   31-61B.

Early morning near Lealholm in the **Esk Valley** Much of Sutcliffe's rural work was done in this locality. The atmospheric haze in the valley contributes strongly to this photograph.

Early photographic plates, being relatively more sensative to the blue end of the spectrum accentuated distance by over-emphasising the amount of ultra-violet light present in a landscape, thus making the photograph appear more hazy than would have been apparent to the human eye.   3-61B.

Evening light on Lealholmside. An incongruous note in the idyllic rural scene is struck by the distant chimney of the ironstone furnace at Glaisdale — long since demolished.   2-61A.

"Darby and Joan". A photographic composition by Frank Sutcliffe which is one of the most satisfying in the collection.   C-27D.

Where no spring or other natural water supply was at hand the saving of rain-water in large butts was a necessity in the absence of a piped main laid to the house. Of interest is what appears to be wooden guttering and fall pipe, an unusual feature locally. The picture as such, speaks for itself.   D-23C.

A three horse team chain harrowing in Foulbriggs Field on Lealholm Hall Farm with Hill House Farm in the background. Sutcliffe took many photographs in this locality.   20-30C.

The tranquility which permeates this picture belies the hard and unremitting toil which characterised 19th century farming life in the Esk Valley.   A-32C.

An intriguing photograph. It is difficult to decide whether this is a 'rigged' studio set or a genuine outdoor shot. The lighting suggests studio — the background suggests otherwise. Whatever . . . . . . it makes up into a powerful composition. The appearance of the whole plate negative suggests that it has been cut down from a larger format.   12-37C.

What an unremarkable subject!
And yet . . . . . . a further study shows the genius of Sutcliffe's "seeing eye". The sense of wild movement — where none in fact exists — is suggested by the chaotic condition of the fence and the wind-swept old fruit trees. We are told that this was taken at the thatched cottage near Glaisdale where Sutcliffe and his family stayed. 6-81A.

An interesting rock formation and a fine photograph. Probably on the River Esk somewhere near Lealholm.   C-46A.

Thomason Foss on the Eller Beck between Goathland and Beckhole approximately eight miles from Whitby.   14-50B.

Four of Frank Sutcliffe's children photographed at Ewe Cote Hall on the outskirts of Whitby. Lying along the branch is Horace, with Kathy on the ladder; Irene is holding the dog and behind her is Zoe, the youngest member of the family.   25-50C.

Picking wild roses at Ewe Cote Hall, Whitby. Two of Frank Sutcliffe's daughters; Lulu (nearest camera) and Zoe. Taken in the early 1900s. 6-77A.

John Ruskin at Brantwood, Coniston in 1872. A wet plate negative, cracked diagonally across the centre, it is most likely one of those which more or less survived the disastrous return journey from Tonbridge Wells in 1876 when many of Sutcliffe's earliest negatives were broken. It has at some time been bound to an additional piece of glass.

Sutcliffe was commissioned by Ruskin to visit him at Brantwood and photograph the house and garden, and this portrait was taken on that occasion.   24-34C.

One of Sutcliffe's earlier photographs — a wet plate probably dating from the mid 1870s. The original negative is in remarkably good condition. A charming picture, made outside the old cottage on the Mulgrave estate.   3-63A.

"Curfew of the Sun". This picture has a cold bleakness, emphasised by the title chosen by Sutcliffe together with the gnarled and leafless oak tree. The skilfully thatched straw rick is worthy of note.   A-10C.

To end our nostalgic journey back into the last century what more fitting than this photograph — probably of one of Sutcliffe's daughters — looking out over Sandsend Bay toward Kettleness below a sunset sky.

Even in this shot the practicalities of everyday life intrude. The low wooden rail on which the girl's foot is resting was a rubbing strip along which a rope could slide when a becalmed boat was being manually towed towards land.   11-40D.